Vegetable Container Gardening

A Quick Start Guide

by Martha Green

http://www.unitedpublishinghouse.com/

Paperback Edition

For information, please contact the author by email at Authors@UnitedPublishingHouse.com.

Other Books by Martha Green

Container Gardening:
A Quick Start Guide

Organic Gardening:
A Quick Start Guide

Green and Clean:
Getting Started with Natural Cleaning

Green and Clean:
Natural Cleaning in the Kitchen

Green and Clean:
Natural Cleaning in Bedrooms and Bathrooms

Green and Clean:
Natural Cleaning in the Laundry Room

Green and Clean:
Natural Cleaning Outside Your Home

Green and Clean:
Homemade Personal Care Products

Green and Clean:
The Ultimate Collection

Table of Contents

Introduction

In my book, ***Container Gardening: A Quick Start Guide,*** I shared extensively about how to pick certain types of containers, the kind of soil to use, types of plants for various sizes of containers, and much more.

In this book, I want to take the practice of container gardening and concentrate on growing vegetables in them. If you read my book on container gardening, you will be familiar with what is discussed in the succeeding chapters. I encourage you to read through the material presented here, even if you have read my other book because there will be some things you may not remember from my other book, and you will discover new information I have included in this one. Ultimately, I want this book to be a complete resource for anyone desiring to grow vegetables in containers, so some repetition from my other book is necessary.

Container gardening is gaining in popularity and much of this is due to people who have never gardened before. Many find success in growing a few vegetables in containers located on their decks, patios, and porches. In addition, much of container gardening's popularity is due to the fact that people's time is limited, yet this form of gardening allows them to spend some of their free time growing vegetation that is satisfying and fruitful.

Others like the flexibility of being able to relocate their containers from outside to inside to take control of the moisture, temperature, sunlight and other needs of a growing plant. Even others who have never tried gardening before but attempt container gardening often do so because it is less intimidating than a garden in the ground and some discover that container gardening is just easier to manage. With these types of advantages, many enjoy the opportunity of having a beautiful, healthy and productive container garden.

As we begin, there are some basic information about container gardening you will need to know. By learning about this type of gardening, your experiences in growing vegetables will be more enjoyable, productive, and hopefully, hassle-free. My hope is you will find the information in this book helpful because it will make good use of your time, maximize your efforts and direct you in ways to save money as you work toward a fruitful container vegetable garden.

What Does Container Gardening Mean?

Container gardens allow you to make any area brighter and more colorful, even when the space is limited in size. You can enjoy growing plants in places where you thought it might be impossible otherwise. Containers placed in corners, suspended from ceilings, window boxes placed on railings, and even small pots placed on a shelf or bookcase are just a few examples for these types of gardens and arrangements.

If you cannot grow a garden outside of your home because of poor soil, if you are living in a limited space without access to an outdoor garden, or if you only have a small deck, you can still enjoy the simple pleasures that container gardening offers.

The increasing popularity of container gardens in different parts of the world has taught many people the benefits of cultivating these masterpieces. You might see plants growing in containers on balconies or rooftops, in office spaces, restaurants, and more. People can create special gardens—regardless of the location or the space available to them. Additionally, individuals find they are able to grow special plants that may require extra attention concerning soil and water—plants they could not manage if they were part of a large garden.

Vegetables and flowers can take on an entirely new look when displayed in a container that highlights their unique shape, size, color, and texture. This offers instant color to a room any time of day, and beautiful displays of plants can often change the entire look of a space. These are some of the reasons why container gardening has become a favorite option incorporated by interior designers when dealing with spaces.

Even if you have enough room in your garden outside for planting, container gardens allow you to tailor your decorations around seasonal changes. For example, if you live in a climate that experiences all four seasons, the winter may deem it necessary to move your containers inside where your plants can be protected. The portability of gardens in containers gives you the option of enjoying your foliage year round—even in an area where the weather changes dramatically.

Container gardening offers the option of allowing you to own a garden. It gives you the flexibility to reorder or move your plants around whenever and wherever you like. You also have the freedom to choose the plants you want to grow, whether they are flowers, vegetables, herbs, or combinations of all three. You can even grow tropical plants during the winter months if you keep the plants inside your home. Then, when the summertime comes, you can either transplant your plants outside or simply move the containers outdoors.

Creating a container garden makes it possible for those who live in the city to enjoy eating fresh salads with the lettuce, tomatoes, and herbs they have grown. High-rise patios and porches become even more beautiful with the addition of container gardens displaying their arrays of brilliant colors and shapes.

Container gardening is extremely versatile, is not difficult to achieve, and actually has several advantages. These are what we will discuss in the next chapter.

What Are Some Advantages of Container Gardening?

Container gardening has many options. From round or rectangular, to tall or short, there are many choices for starting your own beautiful garden—even if it's only for an area of one foot by four feet.

Think for a moment and ask yourself, "Have I ever tried container gardening before?" The answer is probably yes but you may never have thought of your efforts as container gardening. Did you ever bring home a small plant you started in a paper cup while you were in school? Did a friend ever give you an extra tomato plant they did not have room for in their garden? If so, then you have had some experience with container gardens already. Every year millions of people head to their local nursery or home-supply store and stock up on flowers, vegetables, fruits, and herbs to plant at home so they can enjoy the products of their labor weeks and months later.

Container gardening actually has numerous advantages that make it a great option—whether you are just beginning or have been cultivating plants this way for a long time.

1. If you are a beginner, this is a great way to start growing your own plants ~ Almost every experienced gardener will tell you that they have had plants die. This is just part of the process. However, the nice thing about container gardening is it is manageable, allowing you to keep up with what you are growing. Even if you have a busy schedule, most find they are able to successfully grow beautiful gardens at home in containers.

2. The spread of diseases to other plants is less likely to occur ~ Plants can get diseases too, but they are less likely to infect other plants when they are contained in individual pots as opposed to a garden in the ground. It will also be a lot easier for you to treat your plants if they become infested because you can move the container away from the others until the plant either dies or nursed back to health.

3. Maintenance of your container garden will result in less pain for your back ~ You can easily adjust the height of the containers so it is most comfortable for you, unlike regular plants in the ground. Placing containers on tabletops, concrete blocks, or suspending them from railings lets you decide what height best meets your physical needs.

4. Portability is one of the greatest advantages of container gardening ~ With container gardens, you can transfer your plants outdoors or bring them indoors whenever you like. For instance, when your area is about to experience a frost, you can bring your plants inside—that is, if your containers are not too heavy to be moved. If you relocate to a new home or city, containers offer you the opportunity to take your plants along with you.

5. Containers come in many different shapes, sizes, colors and materials ~ Choose containers that best fit your design needs for inside or outside your house. In addition, containers can be changed and used to create unique looks and atmospheres. Whether you are looking for a formal and manicured look, a homey and cottagey style, or flowering plants that create a sense of relaxation, this type of gardening offers many options for you to try.

6. Container gardening is economical ~ It is not necessary, especially for beginners, to invest in expensive containers and tools. You can actually use almost anything as long as you realize there are two basic elements that have to be met:

- First, you want to pick a container that has good drainage.
- Secondly, do your best to make sure that your plants will look great in the containers you choose. Using

pictures from the plant's packaging, try to visualize how the plant's shape and leaf formations will look in the container once they have matured.

If you are just starting out, you can use some containers that you may already possess. Just make sure your container can efficiently get rid of any excess water your plant does not need through drain holes in the bottom. Let your imagination kick in here by using an old pot with some holes in the bottom, a watering can repainted, or a large empty water bottle cut in half.

7. Feeding your plants in containers is a lot easier than feeding plants that live outside ~ Compared to the size of large gardens in the ground, the containers you will be using are relatively small. This means fertilizing and feeding your plants is rather easy and does not require as much product or time. You will find that you will be able to distribute the plant food rather quickly as your containers retain the food you administer.

8. You can extend the growing season of your plants ~ Since you will have more control over the environment your plants live in, you can actually extend their growing season. Even if you don't bring your containers inside, you can keep the soil warm for a longer period of time by insulating and wrapping your pots or containers by wrapping them with towels or thick blankets.

9. Container gardens allow you to showcase beautiful plants ~ As your plants grow and the flowers bloom, containers make it possible to show them off by moving them to places where they can be enjoyed by you and others.

10. Container gardening offers unlimited possibilities ~ You can grow almost any kind of plant in a prepared container. While we all make some mistakes in this area, through trial and error, your efforts are often greatly rewarded with great tasting food and beautiful arrays of flowering plants.

To close out this chapter, I thought it would be helpful to share a few disadvantages of container gardening. Because they offer so many possibilities and options, the disadvantages are rather minimal.

1. Plants that are grown inside containers tend to experience soil drying out quicker than those planted in the ground. Because of this, it is best to water your plants early in the morning or later in the evening when the sun has gone down. This greatly reduces the loss of water through evaporation and helps to minimize any damage that can occur to the plants during the middle parts of the day.

2. Because of a container's limitations in size and confinement, plants are unable to siphon needed water through their root systems from the ground. As a result, watering may need to occur more frequently. In addition, this may result in important nutrients draining from your soil, so you may find it necessary to fertilize your plants more often to replace these nutrients.

3. This one is obvious but deserves a quick mention. Container gardens are limited to the size of the space you have available. However, if you live in an apartment complex and have no yard, container gardens suddenly become a very viable option and an advantage over not being able to grow anything at all.

Hopefully by now, you are beginning to get excited about the possibilities of your own vegetable container garden, so now let's move into a discussion of what you need to get started. This will be covered in the next chapter.

What Do I Need to Get Started?

Now that we have talked about some of the basics of container gardening, let's get started with some of the things you will need. Below is a list of necessary tools you will need to guarantee your success:

Artificial Lighting ~ Indoor container gardens will need light to allow plants and vegetables to grow, especially if they are located in an area without access to direct sunlight or an open window. There are kits you can buy that come with incandescent light bulbs, fluorescent lights and even high-intensity discharge lighting systems. Lighting is an absolute must for seeds to sprout and for plants to grow indoors, even if you plan to transplant them later into an outdoor container.

Tools for Your Soil ~ There are several important tools you will need for your container garden:

- *Hand trowel* ~ The trowel helps you dig a hole in the soil so you can plant your seeds or seedlings. It can also be used to loosen old or hardened soil and is helpful when you add new soil to your containers. You can also use a small handheld miniature rake and hoe to help you cultivate the soil around your plants and to remove weeds that may appear.
- *Soil testers and moisture indicators* ~ These make it easier for you to know when you need to water your plants. A moisture indicator helps you keep from overwatering and to avoid underwatering at the same time.
- *Soil thermometer* ~ This tool enables you to determine if your soil is the right temperature for your plants.

Tools for Watering Your Plants ~ You will need three essential watering tools.

- *Hose-end bubbler* ~ A hose-end bubbler is a tool that you screw onto the end of your garden hose that allows water to be dispensed through multiple holes. This allows for gentler watering of your plants so you do not create holes in your soil as the open end of your hose can do.

- *Watering can* ~ A watering can is one of the most basic watering tools you can have. Like the hose-end bubbler, it lets you water your plants without making deep holes in your soil and causing dirt to splatter. You can also use your watering can to mix up liquid fertilizer and distribute it to your plants gently.
- *Spray bottle* ~ For indoor plants, using a spray bottle to keep your plants well hydrated is a good option, too. Adjust the nozzle so it distributes the water or liquid fertilizer in a gentle mist.

Tools for Grooming Your Plants ~ An additional hand tool you will find extremely helpful is a set of handheld shears or hand pruners. These are used for clipping off dead flowers and old blooms. The hand pruners make it possible for you to clip stems and shoots that may be growing where you do not want them to grow.

When purchasing these hand tools, try to find stainless steel because of its longevity and make sure the handles are well made and strongly attached to the stainless steel, durable, and easy for your hands to hold.

And let us not forget that vegetable plants and seeds are a necessary element for your garden. Because there is much to say about this "tool," it will be covered in extensive detail in later chapters.

Where Can My Garden Grow?

Determining the ideal locations for your vegetable garden containers is essential because they greatly influence the health of the plants. There are some places inside and outside your home where you can easily grow your plants, while other spaces will cause poor results. Below are a few details outlining the most common garden locations, along with the pros and cons of having your plants located there:

Patio/Balcony

Raising your plants on the patio or balcony can be both relaxing and entertaining. It is also one of the best ways to have a garden when your space is limited. You can use hooks to hang old cooking pots that you no longer use to create a place for delicious vegetables. Consider painting them to make them more attractive. There are beautiful hanging baskets you can use, as well as decorative ceramic containers and self-standing pots to bring color and variety to your vegetation and spaces.

Window Boxes

These containers are typically attached underneath windows to create spaces that are both useful and decorative. When using these containers, it is necessary to cover the wood with a plastic bag to keep them from rotting. You also may need to punch holes in the bottom of the boxes so water will drain. It is simple to select a box that matches the style and size of your home's exterior. In addition, learn what plants need sun and which need shade before you mount your boxes. If your windows are shaded by trees, but your plants need sun, window boxes may not work very well for you. Also, make sure you can reach your boxes when watering so your plants don't dry out and die.

Hanging Containers

Hanging containers are extremely decorative, and they can brighten up areas where they are used. You can plant in hanging containers as early as April. You can plant various vegetables in hanging baskets such as rhubarb, tomatoes, lettuce and dwarf beans. With hanging containers, you also have a great deal of variety as to where you locate them. If you have plants that need a lot of sun, you can mount them on your decking or balcony out near the end of the overhangs where they will receive plenty of light. If shade is required, mount them up under the roofing of your deck or porch where they can be protected from the sun.

Various Container Sizes

Varying the size of your containers, the content they are made of, and the shapes (round, square, rectangular) all add to the visual interest you can create with self-standing containers. Whether it's concrete, metal, or ceramic, containers come in all shapes and sizes to add variety to your vegetable garden.

Types and Sizes of Containers for Vegetable Growing

In container gardening, you will have several options to choose from. Some of the types of containers used for growing vegetables are:

- Plastic pots
- Clay pots
- Metallic pots
- Wood pots
- Bushel baskets

- Barrels
- Planter boxes

Choosing the right container for your vegetables does require a bit of know-how. You will need to consider several factors when matching up containers with vegetables.

1. Size ~ Generally, wider, deeper, and larger pots are more useful than smaller ones. Using deeper pots is often necessary because these allow the roots of your vegetables to grow, spread out, and not become cramped. Larger containers also have more capacity to hold or support fully grown crops. Therefore, as you think about choosing containers, think several bigger ones rather than small ones.

Size choices often depend upon the type of vegetables you want to grow. These will usually require a compromise between what you can reasonably move and lift, what your plants will like growing in, and what will be supporting your containers. Container sizes range from window boxes about three feet long, hanging baskets that make use of vertical spaces, tubs and pots that are wide in diameter, to extra-large containers that can hold gallons of soil.

Size is an important factor because if your container is too tall, the soil will often dry out at the top of the container while the soil at the bottom remains wet. If your container is too shallow, the soil will have a difficult time retaining enough water to keep your plants healthy.

Here is a basic "rule of thumb" I use and one that will help you decide which containers to use for your plants: **Plants that will grow to be about two to three feet high will require a container that holds at least three to five gallons of soil.**

For instance, if you are growing large plants like tomatoes, it is recommended that you choose bigger pots that have a large diameter and are deep. This allows the roots of the plants to have enough space to spread out so they are not root bound. Larger containers also make watering and fertilizing your plants easier because there is more surface area.

For certain kinds of vegetables, you will need to make the depth of your container more of a priority than the width. For instance, if you want to grow carrots or radishes, you can grow them in a narrow container, but it has to be deep enough to accommodate the height of the growing plant and the depth of the maturing roots.

While there are basic guidelines concerning sizing, do not be afraid to experiment in this area either. Have fun mixing and matching your plants with their containers. This area gives you a chance to learn from your experiences and to enjoy expressing your personality, creativity, and uniqueness.

I have created a chart for you as an easy reference guide. It has some recommended sizes to use for your containers listed on the left side of the chart with the kinds of vegetables that grow best in those sizes listed on the right.

Container Size	Vegetable Best Suited for Container Size
8" to 12"' diameter 9" deep	Lettuces Beets Radishes Onions Peppers
12" to 16" diameter 11" deep (5 gallon bucket)	Broccoli (1 plant) Peas Snap beans Cabbage (1 plant) Eggplants Brussels sprouts (1 plant) Spinach Tomatoes
12" to 16" diameter 16" deep	Cucumbers Squash Cherry tomatoes Beans Carrots
17" to 18" diameter 15" deep (15 gallon pots)	*Use containers that are larger for multiple plants:* Broccoli (3 plants) Chinese cabbage (3 plants) Brussels sprouts (2 plants) Cabbage (3 plants) Peppers (5 plants)

Not all pots have to be round. Rectangular boxes, oval-shaped containers, and barrels are all container options for growing your vegetables.

Types of Materials for Containers

The materials used in making containers and pots can affect how often you need to water your plants and how long the container will last. Some of the types of materials used in making containers consist of the following:

- Terracotta is very porous and is basically a clay pot that is not glazed. Because of its porousness, moisture evaporates quickly. When using this material, you will need to water often.
- Plastic, which can become brittle after several years of being exposed to the sun, retains moisture quite well.

Plastic holds water longer than clay or ceramic but make sure there is sufficient drainage. If made with resin, it is longer lasting than regular plastic.

- Clay is much nicer looking than plastic containers but loses moisture. Consider placing a plastic container down inside a clay pot that is slightly larger than the plastic one.
- Ceramic pots are clay that has been glazed which makes them not porous like terracotta. They retain moisture longer than several others.
- Fiberglass is more durable and lasts longer than plastic does. It is lightweight and resists cracking and breaking like regular plastic will do. This material can even be painted and because they are lightweight, they are easy to move around.
- Concrete, which is very durable, is also heavy and usually doesn't contain drainage holes. To remedy this, place pieces of broken clay pots in the bottom of the pot before putting in your soil. Then run a long straw along the side of the container from the air pockets created by the broken clay pieces up through the soil to the air at the surface. This will allow evaporation of water trapped in the bottom.
- Stone is sun proof and resists frost but is also very heavy.
- Barrels have thick walls and are great for holding shrubs and small trees. These tend to be difficult to move when filled with soil.

- Galvanized metal is quite cheap and weather resistant. However, it heats up rather quickly on hot summer days, which can harm roots. Consider lining metal pots with plastic sheeting or bubble wrap. This will help to insulate the roots from touching the hot sides of the container.
- Wood needs to be made of cedar or redwood because these are rot resistant. If they are large containers, they will become too heavy to move easily when filled with soil.

Containers made from porous materials such as clay and terracotta can dry out quickly when the weather is warm compared to containers made from plastic or wood. On hot or windy days, you will need to water your plants more frequently if you are using these types of containers. At the same time, containers made from clay that are heavier than many other materials make it possible for them to sustain high winds. This helps prevent your plants and their containers from tipping over—something that can result in damages to both your plants and the containers.

Here are a few we will talk about in a later chapter. I've put an image in here to get you excited about some of the possibilities.

Wooden Barrel
Plastic
Container
Materials
Stone
Limestone
Concrete
Granite
Wooden
Galvanized Metal

Other Creative Ideas for Containers

I have seen so many creative ideas from people when they use containers to grow beautiful flowers and vegetables, but they use interesting and sometimes unusual objects to grow vegetation in.

Although some items would not be practical for growing vegetables, many are. This makes designing your garden fun. By using your imagination, you can not only enjoy the process, but it brings an element of fun into your gardening.

2. Arrangements ~ Below, I have listed some ways you can use items you already own and if you are handy, you have a lot of options.

Make Pot Groupings Appealing

Use containers of different colors and sizes. For instance, you can use one pot that is taller, one that is shorter with a different shape, and one that balances the two pots. Position them in a triangular form and make sure that one container dominates the others. You can even add more pots that are smaller in size around the triangle to make it more appealing. This will make your garden look vibrant and impressively attractive.

Make a Vertical Pallet Garden

This can be made of old wood shipping pallets and can be placed against the fence or wall. You can also make it stand by using strings or supporting it with posts. You can plant vines in the pallet and place it on a balcony. Make sure that you leave it flat on the ground for two weeks to prevent the soil from falling out. This can also hold the plants in place before you hang the wood pallet.

Use Rain Boots and an Old Bicycle

Old rain boots are among the most useful and interesting pots in container gardening. If you have several pairs of boots that you no longer use, you can use them as planters. Plant your crop in each boot and line up all the pairs of rain boots on your fence or stand them on the ground. An old rusty bicycle is also one of the most attractive planters that you can use in your garden. You can use its basket as a container for your crops and plant decorative vines in the bicycle's body.

Reinvent a Wooden Beer Barrel

You can make a few stylish planter designs out of wooden beer barrel. Making a beer barrel as a planter is easy whether you place it indoors or outdoors. Beer barrels are excellent embellishments especially when it's placed in the garden outdoors. You can let it stand whole as a planter or cut it in half vertically. You can line up the cut wooden beer barrel in your garden or just use one in the porch.

Garden Pots and Wine Boxes on the Wall

This is another simple design that can create a sophisticated appearance on your garden. Purchase gardening pots that have the same color and size. Plant the crops first, then hang them on the wall in a symmetrical arrangement. You can plant herbs and seasonal crops in this garden design. You can also make use of your wine boxes and hang them vertically on the wall indoors. You may use hooks and wires to connect each box and vertically position them 1 foot apart from each other.

Decorate Using Old Furniture

Using old furniture such as a dresser is one brilliant way to beautify your garden. You can reuse the entire dresser or just the dresser drawer as a container. It can add a wonderful charm in your garden outdoors or the patio especially when you grow some edible flowers in it. You can also reuse a garden bench or a chair and make them as planters. You only need to repaint them to add more character to your outdoor container garden. An old chair can be a very appealing plant stand especially if it looks really old.

Wheelbarrow Mini Garden

Use an old wheelbarrow as a container for your garden. You just need to make sure that there are holes at the bottom surface of the cart for drainage. Adding stones is also one good way to improve the drainage system of the soil. You can grow vegetable varieties that have the same growing needs in the wheelbarrow. This will make a really nice addition to your container garden outdoors.

Recycle Kids' Garbage

Look for a vintage baby stroller and use it as a decorative planter indoors. It is not just easy to use and move because of its wheels, but it is also ornamental when placed in the porch or inside the house. You can also use baby bathtub, paddling pool and a toy dump truck as planters. If you have kick balls in the basement, make them as hanging baskets. You can even repaint them to match the color of your home.

Make a Chandelier Garden

There are actually two ways to come up with a chandelier garden. You can create a chandelier garden yourself or buy an old chandelier. This can be a great idea if you are bored with hanging baskets or hanging containers on the wall. Create your own chandelier by using pots with the same size and shape, and then using a wire to hang them from above. The pots should be close with each other to make a chandelier. You can also reuse your old chandelier or buy one at auction stores. You can replace the candleholders with pots or mugs and make them as planters.

3. Shape ~ The shape of a container can contribute to its stability and is an important aspect to consider. If the area you live in is susceptible to strong winds, square-shaped containers often prove to be more stable than rounder ones. A shape such as this helps keep your container from tipping over during strong winds or breezes, preserving both your plants and containers from being damaged. Using different shapes also adds variety to the form of your garden, as well as visual interest.

4. Weight ~ Soil can be very heavy, so if you choose a container that is heavy as well, it can be very difficult to move around your deck or patio, as well as from indoors to outdoors. When choosing a container, consider the extra weight that the plants, soil and water will create. This is especially important if you plan to change the look of your garden on a regular basis by moving them around very often and very far. While it may be necessary to choose heavier containers because you want to grow taller plants that need stability, try to stick with lightweight materials for these plants. In addition, consider mounting heavy containers on low platforms that have wheels.

5. Maintenance ~ If you have a limited amount of time to care for your garden or you simply want caring for it to be a low maintenance affair, choose pots made from materials that will not need restoring from time to time. Containers made from wood usually need to be treated on a regular basis with a preservative or a stain to maintain their quality and appearance, as well as preventing them from deteriorating due to various weather conditions. Options like stone and fiberglass can be great choices for carefree maintenance.

6. Price ~ This is another important factor to consider because the containers you buy could greatly impact the budget you have allotted for your garden. You do have the option of reusing or recycling several different types of containers rather than buying new and expensive ones every year; however, the start-up costs can be substantial if you aren't careful.

As you can see from the information in this chapter, there are many things to think about when trying to pick containers for your garden. While there are important things to consider, this is such fun for me because of the many choices there are and for the chance to express some of my personality. I hope you find this to be true for you as well.

Now that we've talked about the containers themselves, let us move on to another facet of your garden with many options—the plants you want to grow in your new containers.

Planning What to Grow and When

One of the nicest things about container gardening with vegetables is you can grow food all year long; however, there are certain guidelines you will want to follow. If you want to plant vegetables like broccoli, peas, and carrots, you will want to plant them in the spring or fall. However, if cucumbers, summer squash and tomatoes get you excited, then once the danger of frost is over, then you can plant so many things.

Obviously, if you are like me, you enjoy planting a variety of vegetables. This means some will be planted in the spring, while others can be started in the fall. Because not everything is started at the same time, it is important to plan what you want to grow so you will know when to plant your vegetables.

Along with planting a variety of vegetables, as I have shared with you before, vegetables vary in their needs. Some need shallow soil while others need room for their roots to spread out.

In this chapter, I want to try and give you some guidelines of when to plant certain vegetables and what they will need to thrive. This will help you to decide what you need to think about and purchase for a fruitful growing season.

In the chart below, I have tried to give you an overview of some of the most popular vegetables people like to grow. It gives the name of the vegetable, when to plant, when to harvest, and minimum depth of the container to allow healthy growth. Please note: In the column that says, "When to Plant," this means actually planting a young plant into the soil. If you decide to start your plants from seeds, you will need to begin that process several weeks earlier. Be sure to consult the seed's packaging.

Vegetable Planning Calendar

Spring		
What to grow	**When to plant**	**When to harvest**
Arugula	Late spring	Late summer
Beans	Late spring	Late summer
Beets	Early spring	Early summer
Broccoli	Early spring	Late spring - Early summer
Cabbage	Late spring	Early fall
Carrots	Early spring	Early summer
Cauliflower	Late spring	Late summer - Late fall
Collard greens	Early spring	Early summer - Late summer
Corn	Late spring	Late summer - Early fall
Cucumber	Late spring	Late summer - Early fall
Garlic	Early spring	Late summer
Kale	Early spring	Late fall - Early winter
Lettuces	Late spring	Late summer
Mustard greens	Early spring	Early summer - Late summer

Onions (bulbs)	Early spring	Early fall
Peas	Early spring	Late summer
Potatoes	Early - Late spring	Late summer - Late fall
Radishes	Early spring	Late spring - Early summer
Shallots	Early spring	Late summer
Spinach	Early spring	Early summer - Early fall
Tomatoes	Late spring	Late summer - Early fall
Turnip greens	Early spring	Early summer - Late summer
Zucchini	Late spring	Early summer

Summer

What to grow	When to plant	When to harvest
Beets	Early summer	Early fall
Cabbage	Early summer	Late fall
Carrots	Early summer	Early fall
Corn	Early summer	Early fall
Eggplant	Early summer	Early summer - Late summer
Peas	Early summer	Early fall - Late fall

Peppers	Early summer	Late summer - Early fall
Squash	Early summer	Late summer - Early fall
Sweet potatoes	Early summer	Late fall
Tomatoes	Early summer	Early fall - Late fall
Zucchini	Early summer	Late summer

Fall

What to grow	When to plant	When to harvest
Arugula	Late summer - Early fall	Late fall
Broccoli	Early fall	Late fall - Early winter
Cauliflower	Early fall	Late fall - Early winter
Collard greens	Late summer - Early fall	Late fall - Early winter
Kale	Early fall	Early winter
Lettuces	Early fall	Early winter
Mustard greens	Early fall	Early winter
Radishes	Early fall	Late fall
Spinach	Early fall	Early winter - Late winter

If you notice from the chart, there are numerous vegetables you can plant both in the spring and in the fall, making it possible for you to enjoy some of your favorites throughout most of the year.

Here are some additional factors to consider when choosing the plants for your containers:

1. Determine which plants will fit in your available space.

2. Consider whether or not you will have to move your plants around or not. Large and heavy containers are much more difficult to handle than smaller ones.

3. Make sure your plants are suitable for the climate you live in. For instance, there are plants that need direct sunlight on a daily basis while others require indirect or filtered sunlight.

4. Think about choosing plants that have similar needs to each other. This means balancing watering needs with the size of the pot, the types of containers you use, soil types, and the size of vegetation you are growing.

5. Finally, think about your lifestyle. Your habits and routine as a gardener should allow you time to care for your plants. Do not take on more than you have time to handle.

Vegetables Right from the Pot

As you have seen, there are many different kinds of vegetables you can raise in containers. Below is a short description and a picture for some of the most popular vegetables people enjoy growing at home.

Tomatoes

By Martha Green

Tomatoes tend to be one of the vegetables people grow in containers when they first start gardening. Here are a few important things to know about tomatoes:

1. If you decide to grow them, plant them in a large container that is at least fourteen inches in diameter. Additionally, when larger pots are used, tomato plants often respond by getting bigger and producing more fruit.

2. When buying soil for your containers, make sure they are labeled appropriately for larger pots. These will contain ingredients like perlite, composted pine bark, peat moss, rice hulls, coconut pieces, and peanut shells to give your soil some bulk. Avoid mixtures that are high in peat moss because these will cause compression of your soil, thus causing the plant's root mass to be reduced.

3. You will need a vertical support system, like a small trellis. This should be installed around your tomato plant soon after planting so you do not damage your plant as it grows.

4. Never overwater your tomatoes and be sure to keep the soil moist instead of wet. You cold use self-watering containers to make sure that the plant gets the water it needs.

5. You will want to feed your plants with a slow-release fertilizer and provide it with at least six to eight hours of sunlight every day. It is best to plant tomatoes in the

late spring as this lessens their chances of being damaged from frosts.

6. Harvesting tomatoes when they are red means they have reached maturity and are ready to be enjoyed.

Peppers

If you decide to grow peppers, which are also quite popular, strive to find varieties that are labeled, “intended for containers” or “compact.” This means these varieties tend not to grow as big as regular varieties meant for in-ground gardens. Here are some helpful facts to know about peppers:

1. Peppers don’t require too much space to grow. You can grow them in containers starting at nine inches in diameter and about nine inches deep.

2. You will want to buy soil that is labeled for larger containers because this includes bulk materials like pine bark, peanut shells and other hulls which will help keep the soil from becoming too dense. Also, make sure the soil remains moist, even when its surface becomes dried out.

3. Be sure to supply trellis support for your peppers so when they become tall, they will not become damaged by falling over.

4. You can feed it with fertilizer once every week and cover the soil with mulch so it will retain moisture.

5. Sunlight exposure should be direct in the morning and filtered all day long as the afternoon sun can actually burn the crop.

6. Peppers are usually grown during early spring.

7. The peppers are ready to pick when their color and size have reached maturity.

Beans

Beans are another vegetable easily grown in containers. Beans are tasty, easy to grow, and they freeze well, too. Here are a few recommendations if you decide to grow your own:

1. You will need a container about twelve inches wide. If you are growing bush beans, the container depth should be six to seven inches, whereas pole beans require a depth closer to eight or nine inches.

2. With several varieties, you will need to provide a trellis for the plant to grow up on to support the weight of the plant.

3. Consider using pasteurized soil (soil that has been baked in the oven), mix it with compost, and add mulch to help retain the soil's moisture.

4. Make sure you place your containers in a warm or brightly lit location but avoid direct sunlight.

5. You may need to water the beans frequently to keep the soil moist, too.

6. You can plant your seedlings in the spring once the soil has warmed up.

7. When the pods are fully elongated and are crisp and firm, it is time to harvest them. When they reach maturity, be sure to harvest them every day. Frequent harvesting will encourage more beans to be produced from your plant.

Squash/Zucchini

Squash and zucchini fall into the cucurbit category of plants (as do cucumbers). These may not be vegetables you think of right away for growing, but they are not difficult to do and are delicious straight from the garden—raw or cooked. Here are several guidelines to be aware of:

1. Cucurbit plants can be grown in any container that is twelve inches in diameter. Two plants are easily grown side by side in a fourteen-inch-diameter container.

2. Choose a good quality potting soil and mix it with organic matter before planting your seedlings.

3. Make sure your plants get at least eight hours of sunlight per day and be sure to water them often. Do more watering if your container is made of clay rather than plastic because this type of container can cause the soil to dry out faster.

4. Begin to fertilize your plants with a timed-release formula after the first real leaves begin to appear.

5. Plant your seedlings in early to mid summer. This variety of plants are actually very easy to start from seeds, taking about three to four weeks before it is time to transplant into containers. However, many like me just plant the seeds directly into the containers.

6. Depending upon the varieties you choose, cucurbits begin to ripen after 45 days. Consider starting new plants four to six weeks after your initial planting to keep produce fresh throughout the summer.

7. Winter squashes will be ready to harvest about 100 days after planting. If you planted summer squashes, you can pick them when the fruits become about eight inches long and three inches in diameter.

Cucumbers

Because cucumbers are in the cucurbit family, much of what I stated above applies here as well.

1. You need to use a large container that has a diameter of at least 12 inches.
2. Cucumbers need loose soil that reaches 70 degrees Fahrenheit and has good drainage.
3. They also need organic fertilizer to sustain their nutritional needs.
4. Cucumbers are plants that need eight hours of direct exposure to sunlight.
5. Harvest your cucumbers when they are about seven to nine inches long.

Lettuces

Lettuces fall into four different categories: Loose Leaf, Romaine (also known as Cos), Butterheads, and Crisphead. While each has their own characteristics, there are some similarities between them:

1. It is best to plant lettuce seeds directly into a six- to twelve-inch-diameter container that you want them to grow in. They do not transplant well. They only take about one week to germinate and make sure your plants are eight to ten inches apart.

2. Lettuces tend to grow best in cooler temperatures.

3. Use a standard soil mix formulated to provide nutrients and one that will hold moisture. You can mix the soil with compost to make it even healthier.

4. These vegetables grow very successfully in containers, enabling you to keep pests, snails and slugs under control.

5. Do not place these vegetables in direct sunlight. Instead, place them in a shady place for best results.

6. Lettuces need to be harvested within a week of when they are ready or the leaves will begin to bolt. When this happens, a flower stalk will appear, will go to seed, and the leaves become bitter tasting. Therefore, plant only the amount you plan to use.

7. The plant itself grows quickly, especially when soil conditions are healthy.

8. Be sure your containers drain well but also make sure the soil remains moist.

9. Lettuce plants require little to no fertilizer, if you are using good soil.

10. Lettuces will be ready to harvest anywhere from eight to fourteen weeks.

11. The best method for enjoying lettuce throughout the growing season is to plan to sow a few lettuce seeds every two weeks. Then, when you harvest the lettuce, be sure to put up the whole plant. This will discourage diseases in the ground and rotting.

Potatoes

By Martha Green

Potatoes come in so many beautiful colors like blue, yellow, purple, and read as well as various shapes. Growing potatoes in containers is slightly different from other vegetables but they can grow quite successfully. In fact, growing them in containers actually minimizes problems with contaminates in the soil and susceptibility to pests. Here are some overall guidelines:

1. Use a deep container to grow your potatoes in because they need depth in order to mature. Consider using one that is fourteen to sixteen inches deep and has good drainage.

2. While potatoes are available at many gardening and nursery centers, it is also possible to grow potatoes using potatoes bought from the grocery store. However, make sure they are organically grown because some potatoes have been chemically treated so they won't produce "eyes"—a necessary element for growing them. In addition, consider ones that have signs of sprouting.

3. For the soil, use potting soil with multipurpose compost and an organic fertilizer.

4. Potato pieces with eyes are placed on top of a few inches of soil, then covered with about six inches of soil. As the plant grows upward, additional soil is added—about a shovel full every two weeks.

5. These plants need moist soil, so be sure the soil does not dry out.

6. Place the potatoes in an area where it is partially shaded and partially exposed to sunlight. They require about six to eight hours of sunlight each day. Direct sunlight for long periods of the day is not good for these plants.

7. Different varieties of potatoes will determine when to plant them, ranging from February to as late as July.

8. Start harvesting when the leaves begin to turn brown and die—anywhere from two to four months from planting.

Radishes

Radish is a vegetable that provides a spicy taste to salads and it is not difficult to grow. While they grow quickly, there are a few things you need to know about growing them:

1. Because radishes have a small root system, they can grow in shallow containers and you can plant seeds two to three inches apart. Different varieties of radishes will require different depths, ranging anywhere from six to twelve inches.

2. Radishes tolerate numerous types of soil. Use soil-less multipurpose compost and cover the base with moisture-retaining materials such as pebbles and old shards. Also, be sure the soil remains loosely packed and keep the soil clumps small.

3. Radishes should get plenty of sunlight exposure, and it is best to place them in a semi-shaded or sunny location.

4. Radishes can be planted during the spring and fall, and your radishes are ready to harvest in as little as three weeks.

5. The biggest challenge with radishes is keeping slug away from them. This can easily be accomplished by placing a circle of rock salt around the periphery of the radish container.

6. Because of their rapid growth, it is possible to keep planting and harvesting all throughout the year.

Eggplant

Eggplant is a vegetable that grows very well, especially if you purchase ones that are labeled "compact" for containers. There are several other guidelines you will want to know about before growing these:

1. Each plant needs to be planted in containers twelve to fourteen inches in diameter to thrive and up to three plants can be planted in the same container if you use a pot that is at least twenty inches in diameter.

2. Use a mixture of potting soil and sand to ensure that the plant gets the nutrients and moisture it needs.

3. You should plan to feed your plant on a weekly basis with a soluble fertilizer.

4. Some varieties will need a short support system. Two to three ringed supports used for tomatoes work well. Be sure to install them right after planting so you don't damage your plant trying to put them in after the plant has grown significantly.

5. Make sure to allow your plant to get eight hours of direct sunlight and keep the soil moist at all times.

6. For most temporal climates, eggplant should not be planted until early April because these plants need a warmer growing environment.

7. You will know when the eggplant is ready for harvest once its skin becomes glossy. You can also test for ripeness by pressing into the eggplant's skin with your

finger, and if it doesn't spring back, it is ready for your table.

Carrots

If you decide to try your hand at growing carrots at home, I think you will definitely enjoy the results. Let me share a couple of things you will need to know to get started:

1. Carrots come in various varieties. Strive to find ones that don't require a lot of depth. Chantenay and Nantes are two such kinds.

2. When choosing a container, use a round one that is approximately thirteen inches in diameter and twelve inches deep. If you use a window box, use one that is approximately twenty-two inches long, eight inches wide, and eight inches deep. For square, use twelve inches wide by thirteen inches deep.

3. You can begin planting carrot seeds as early as March.

4. You can use a soil mixture or soil-less medium, ensuring that it drains well.

5. Use more seeds than plants because you will thin them out as they grow.

6. Because birds like the taste of young carrot plants, you will need to cover your containers in the beginning with netting or wire.

7. Carrot plants tend to sprout within a week after planting the seeds. Once your plants come through the surface, you will eventually want to thin them out, resulting in each plant being two to three inches apart.

8. They need full sunlight for about six hours a day in order to grow, with partial shade as well.

9. Harvesting can occur approximately sixty to eighty days after planting.

We have talked about what kind of containers you might buy and the kinds of plants you could grow. Now it is time to address another important topic—soil. What goes into your containers may surprise you so let's get right into this "life support" system for your plants in the next chapter.

What Type of Soil Do I Use?

Having good quality soil is one of the most essential parts of container gardening. The basic purpose of the soil for your containers and plants is to help with retention of moisture, to support the structure of your plants, to bring air to their roots, and to maintain nutrients necessary for your plant's health.

When choosing to grow vegetation in containers, you will find that your traditional ways of thinking about soil have to change. Container gardening requires soils that can drain well and are able to aerate well—all while being able to hold on to and retain the moisture necessary for your plants to grow.

The first rule to know when preparing soil for your containers is this: **Do not use regular soil from your yard or garden, even if it looks great and things have grown well in this dirt before.** Garden soil from the ground is too heavy and actually "too dirty" for using in containers; however, it can be a part of a container mix as will be shown later in this chapter. The rules change when you go from yard gardens to those in containers because the ability for air to reach your plants and their drainage are greatly affected. Ignoring this fact will cause your plants to have poor outcomes or they may even die.

It is interesting to note that these types of soils actually do not contain soil at all. In fact, they are referred to as soil mixtures, potting soil, container mix, artificial media, and some even include the word soil-less. These mixtures are well aerated, sterile, and lightweight. They contain an excellent balance of organic materials and mineral particles such as peat, sand and perlite. Since they are soil-less, this means they will not have any dirt in them.

Different manufacturers offer various recipes for container soils but in a nutshell a good mix will consist of one part vermiculite, one part potting soil, one part compost, and one part sphagnum peat moss. If you don't have compost, you can add a fertilizer that slowly releases nutrients.

Many mixes for containers begin with organic materials. While there are too many to mention here, some of the basic ones include pine bark, compost, husks from coconuts (also known as coir), and peat.

Because drainage and the ability for air to penetrate the soil are two of the biggest factors in your plant's health, many soil mixtures will contain sand, polystyrene, and perlite. These materials are especially helpful for keeping the weight of heavier soil mixes to a minimum.

So, how do you know which soil to choose? If you are a beginner, the easiest way to start is to buy soil mixtures that are specifically labeled for container gardens. This almost guarantees that you have made the right choice. If you want to try your hand at creating some of your own mixtures as you feel more confident, here are just a few combinations you can try that have brought me good results:

- 1 part perlite: 3 parts peat moss
- 2 parts peat moss: 1 part coconut husks (coir)
- 1 part sand: 1 part garden soil: 1 part peat moss
- 1 part sand: 1 part peat moss: 3 parts hardwood bark
- 1 part perlite: 2 parts pine bark: 2 parts vermiculite
- 1 part perlite: 1 part vermiculite: 2 parts peat moss

Because you have limited the amount of soil mixture to the size of your containers, this means your containers only contain a limited amount of nutrients. It will be necessary for you to supply a regular amount of nutrients for your plants.

You can add fertilizers to the soil that are slowly absorbed and are added before you fill up your containers. This makes food readily available for your plants. Additional food can be added if desired from the top, guaranteeing your plants receive a steady supply of nutrients. There are pre-mixed fertilizers you can buy that make this option affordable and easy.

Finally, it is possible to reuse soil year after year, but as a beginner, I would advise you not to. Many of the nutrients will have been depleted by the end of your plant's growing season. Additionally, soil that has "aged" can be prone to insects, fungus, and diseases. It would be best to invest in a new round of potting mixtures.

However, as you gain experience, you may want to try your hand at reusing your soil. You can revitalize some of your old soil with additional nutrients. This can be done by removing some of the old soil and replacing it with new. Another option would be to learn how to sterilize your old soil. This process is outlined in the chapter entitled, "How Do I Manage Pests and Diseases?"

Now it's time to talk about nourishing your plants once you have planted them in the soil. I'm referring to the topic of fertilizing your plants and this will be discussed in the next chapter.

How Do I Feed My Garden So It Can Feed Me?

Fertilizers are among the most important things that you need to have and use if you are growing a garden. There are fertilizer options to choose from, and they vary according to their ingredients, nutritional benefits and other factors. There are also various techniques that are used to ensure that you are feeding your plants properly.

Fertilizing My Vegetables

When you frequently water your plants, the nutrients in the soil normally leach out. Fertilizers can supply the soil and plant with the nutrients they need, especially when you have to supply a lot of water to your containers. Fertilizers are food for plants, and they provide your garden plants with the nutrients they need to survive and grow.

There are basically two kinds of fertilizers—inorganic and organic. Inorganic fertilizers deliver food to your plants quickly whereas organic ones do this slowly. Organic fertilizers are created from living organisms and, as such, bring fungi and bacteria to your soil, as well as texture—inorganic does not. Some of the organic types of fertilizers consist of worm manure, compost, and seaweed. Be sure to purchase these from a reputable dealer before adding to your containers.

Inorganic fertilizers are chemical additives. Usually available in two forms—liquids and solids—these supply ingredients like potassium, calcium, zinc, nitrogen, and other important nutrients to your plants. Solid fertilizers tend to release nutrients slowly over time while liquids feed your plants much quicker.

Choose the Right Fertilizers

Because your plants cannot obtain the nutrients they might otherwise get from the natural environment, you need to provide adequate nutrition to your plants by choosing the right fertilizer.

A slow-release fertilizer normally supplies the plant with nutrients for 60 to 120 days. It works by releasing nutrients once it comes in contact with water. This means that every time you water your plant, you are automatically fertilizing it.

You can assist the efficiency of the slow-release fertilizer by applying **a water-soluble fertilizer** as well. This product will take care of delivering the nutrients to the roots of your plants. A water-soluble fertilizer is normally dissolved in water and poured into the container.

There are also **spray water-soluble fertilizers** you can use to aid stressed plants. You can cut the damaged parts of the plants and spray the fertilizer. This will allow the nutrients to go directly into the plant and can result in the plant's dramatic growth and renewal.

One of the secrets in feeding your containerized plants is to **use controlled-release granular fertilizer**. You can use this when you plant your plants or sprinkle it over the soil's surface. Controlled-release fertilizers are able to provide the nutritional needs of your plants even without the use of soluble fertilizers. Choose a product that contains appropriate amounts of potassium, phosphorus and nitrogen.

You may want to consider using organic fertilizers as these can significantly help increase the plant's protection from pests. This type of fertilizer can also make your vegetables more nutritious, flavorful and aromatic.

Know the Signs of the Plant's Nutritional Deficiencies and How to Fertilize

Certain symptoms normally appear when a plant experiences nutritional deficiencies. These symptoms are your plant's way of communicating to you what it needs. Knowing about these symptoms will also help you understand and determine what the best fertilizers for your plants are. Look at the details below to see how certain nutritional deficiencies manifest themselves in the plant's appearance:

- Calcium deficiency – This deficiency will display symptoms such as leaf discoloration and brown spots.

- Nitrogen and sulfur deficiency – Stunted plant growth and its older leaves will appear lighter than the young leaves.
- Phosphorus deficiency – This condition also exhibits discoloration symptoms. Most often, the top side of the old leaves will turn dark green and the bottom part turns red.
- Potassium deficiency – This impedes water absorption in plants and the growth of new tissues. The plant normally dies when it suffers from this deficiency.

If containerized plants are not given time-release fertilizer, you will need to feed them once every two weeks with water-soluble fertilizer. During midway through the growing season, you can treat your crops with liquid fertilizer about once a week. This is essential for your plants during this time because this is normally when they start producing their fruit.

If you are raising root vegetables, feed them with fertilizers that are rich in phosphorus. However, if you are growing leaf vegetables, use fertilizers that are nitrogen-rich. When you are watering your plants on a daily basis, you need to provide your vegetables with liquid fertilizer once a week, especially when the weather is hot or dry. You can apply the liquid fertilizer every other week if you don't irrigate frequently or when the weather is cool. Always remember to follow the instructions provided on the fertilizer's label.

Things You Should Not Do When Fertilizing

1. You should not sprinkle too much granular fertilizer in the soil because this can cause burning of your plants.

2. Avoid fertilizing plants that are dried, sick or wilted. Instead, water them and then treat them with a water-soluble fertilizer. Only use this treatment once you see the plants are well watered and have recovered.

3. Avoid overfeeding your plants because it will not speed up their growth. When you apply amounts of fertilizer that are more than the suggested dosage, or when you use it longer than recommended, it can be fatal to your plants.

Watering My Plants

Nourishing your containerized crops with water is as necessary as fertilizing them. If your plants don't get the right amount of water they need, it can negatively affect your harvest. Container soil dries out faster than garden soil, which is exactly why you need to water your plants regularly. Watering can vary depending on the type of plant and container, the duration of time the crop has been planted, the location of the container as well as the time of the year such as in summer or fall.

If you are residing in a place with a hot climate, water your plants every day, especially if you are growing root vegetables. Check the dryness or moisture of the soil by sticking a few inches of your finger down into it. If the container is manageable, you can also lift the container, and if it feels too light, it probably means the soil is dry.

Strive to make sure that the root ball of your plants is wet but be careful not to overwater the soil.

One thing that is important to learn about is how to keep your soil moist. While this may sound simple, it actually requires some practice. Drying of soil can happen quickly because pots dry out. The soil then becomes hard and getting it moist again can prove difficult.

If the soil ever dries out, water will run right through it instead of being absorbed. One way to avoid this is to consider using an irrigation system that drips water into your pots for three to four minutes at a time, two to three times each day.

A good rule of thumb to follow concerning watering is this: **water on a regular basis, and then water some more.** This is especially important when the weather conditions are dry. You want to water your plants until you start to see water dripping out of the drainage holes. Once this happens, you should stop so you do not make the soil soggy. If you know you can't water on a regular basis because you travel or have time constraints, consider containers that allow self-watering or use irrigation systems that will water automatically and place these systems on a timer.

Proper Drainage

Proper drainage is another component that is important when watering your plants. When purchasing containers at the store or using ones you have readily available, make sure they have enough drainage holes. Lack of drainage holes can make the soil extremely wet and result in the death of your plants. Choose a container that has eight to ten drainage holes or drill these holes in the bottoms of your containers.

Even when your vegetables are thriving with good nutrition and things are progressing along smoothly, pests and diseases can become issues you have to deal with. These two topics will be addressed in the next chapter.

How Do I Manage Pests and Diseases?

No matter what you do, there will always be pests and diseases to contend with, whether growing plants in an outdoor garden or indoors inside of containers. While these can never be totally eliminated, there are some things you can do and should be aware of to help keep pests and diseases to a minimum.

1. Regularly inspect your containers ~ Containers such as wooden planters can become weak over time, thus inviting pests like sow bugs and ants to come reside in them. As a result, they often damage your container more than the plant. When you see them present, remove them as soon as possible. Pests like these can do extensive damage, sometimes making it necessary to transplant your plants to a different container.

Pests such as earwigs and beetles are notorious for eating the leaves on your plants and then they hide under the containers. Hence, be sure to check under your containers regularly and remove them promptly.

2. Regularly inspect your plants ~ Be sure to check your vegetation for damage from insects. This will allow you to find what pests are causing the damage, remove them quickly, and prevent your plants from suffering major damage. You should be on the lookout for pests like snails and slugs. An easy trick for eliminating them is to simply place pieces of eggshells on the top of the soil. These pests find it extremely difficult to crawl over the rough surfaces and they will end up leaving.

Other pests such as aphids can be removed using strong sprays of water, followed by soapy water sprayed on bugs that are difficult to eliminate.

3. Get to know the pests commonly living in your area ~ While this will take some time to learn, this can prove to be time well spent. Some bugs are actually beneficial to you because they help get rid of the bad kind of pests. This means, if you don't know your bugs, you may end up eliminating the ones that you want to keep around. These good critters feed on bad insects such as aphids, as well as certain insects and pests.

4. Purchase new soil each year or sterilize the soil you plan to reuse ~ Diseases such as fungi and some insects can reside in the soil and debris in and around your containers. If your budget allows, purchase new soil each year when the time to start your garden comes. If money is tight, you could consider sterilizing the soil you already own; however, while it is cheaper to reuse your soil, it can be an extensive process.

Sterilizing soil involves the following steps:

- Use a large roasting pan and bag. With about five cups of soil placed in the roasting bag, a cup of water is mixed in with the soil. The bag is placed into the pan with the top left open to allow moisture to escape.
- You will need an oven thermometer. Stick the thermometer through the bag and turn the oven on to a low temperature.
- Heat the oven not hotter than 180 degrees F. Heated soil will produce some very unpleasant odors. You will want to make sure you have good ventilation when you attempt this.
- The process takes about 30 minutes. When the thermometer reaches 170 degrees, turn the oven down even more. The goal is to remain around 170 degrees for 30 minutes. This will be enough to sterilize your soil. If the temperature of the soil goes over 180 degrees, you will need to discard the soil. This temperature and higher ones create toxic substances in the soil that might kill your plants.

5. Make sure the plants you have chosen to grow are native to your area ~ Some plants are more susceptible to pests and diseases than others, so it is especially important to avoid planting non-native types of plants in your containers. While some plants have managed to acquire their own natural resistance, many will fall prey to pests and diseases if they are not normally grown in your climate.

6. Know your soil ~ Be sure to check the soil in your containers regularly. Not only is it important to know if the soil is moist or dry, but you also want to dig down a little into the soil to check for bugs burrowed in the soil. Regular inspection will ward off infestation, making the solution easier to obtain.

In addition, as you are inspecting the soil, be sure to remove dead leaves and any diseased-looking material from the container. This small act will help eliminate numerous possible breeding grounds for pests and diseases.

If you discover you have a definite problem with pests and diseases, it may be necessary to take definitive action using sticky traps, insecticidal soaps and botanical pesticides. As a last resort, consider synthetic pesticides and chemicals. If these measures become necessary, strive to treat your specific problem and apply the solution on the affected areas only.

7. Make sure your purchased plants are pest-free ~ When choosing plants, make sure that what you purchase are pest-free. If you accidentally purchase an infested plant, you may find it difficult or even impossible to get rid of the pests or diseases.

8. Maintain cleanliness in your garden ~ Get rid of dead plants as they can be a breeding ground for different pests and diseases.

9. Eliminate unhealthy plants from your containers ~ One of the best ways to protect your plants from pesky insects is to apply fertilizers that can help keep your plants healthy and less susceptible to various infestations. When your plant is nutrient-deficient, it becomes weak and can attract pesky insects. If there are weak plants, remove them instantly because they may be infected and susceptible to attracting pests.

A Few Treatment Methods

Because you are growing foods that you and your family will eat, it is best to think about organic and safe methods in treating pests and diseases. Below are just a few suggestions you can try:

- Soft-bodied insects – Eliminate mealybugs, mites and aphids by spraying a mixture of Ivory soap, canola oil and water. You can also use mineral oil, neem oil or hot peppers to burn insects.
- Mites and other insects – You can make a spray bottle solution consisting of hot pepper sauce, Ivory soap and water.

- Fungal diseases – Create a mixture from baking soda and water. Spray the mixture on the affected plants until the fungal diseases disappear.
- Flying insects – Use garlic or onions and liquefy them in a vegetable oil tea.
- Snails and Slugs – Sprinkle crushed egg shells or lime in the soil area where the pests live.
- Fire ants and similar pests – Use citrus acid and molasses or a mixture of garlic and boiling water.
- Japanese beetles – Create a mixture out of water, liquid soap, canola oil and molasses. Pour the mixture in a can and place a rotten fruit in it. This creates a great trap for unwanted beetles.

It is important to note that these sprays do not just kill harmful insects, but also the good ones. Make sure that you use them selectively, and only spray the affected areas. It is also wise to spray in the morning and after a rain shower.

- If you are dealing with gnats, then it is wise to refrain from watering your crops for a while. Gnats cannot survive without water, and if you starve them, they will see your crop unfit for dwelling and disappear.
- If the stems and leaves of your crops are infested with bugs, you can cut them off. Prune the infested areas and throw them away. Some plants have the capacity to recover and sprout again regardless of how extreme your pruning is.

- Using flypapers is one of the best remedies to combat whiteflies and aphids. You can buy flypaper and use them to get rid of the insects. You can also make flypaper by using a yellow board that's coated with an adhesive. This will help eliminate a variety of pests that will be attracted to the board's color.
- You can also get rid of pesky insects by hand picking. Although this method is slow, it is extremely safe. You can do manual handpicking or use a handheld vacuum to get rid of pests.

Finally, I want to share with you some common mistakes involved in gardening. I will share them with you in the next chapter.

What Are Some Common Mistakes I Should Know About?

Face the fact that you are going to make mistakes with container gardening. I've certainly made my share of them so I want to give you some of the most common ones gardeners make so you will know what to expect. Maybe you will do better than I did on my first attempts. Even though I experienced my share of mishaps, I still love container gardening as it is extremely rewarding and can become addictive.

Here is a list to make you more aware and better informed as a gardener as you tend your garden:

1. When dealing with large heavy containers, you wait for the end of the process before moving your pots ~ Do not make the mistake of filling up a large container with soil and your new plants and then try to move it. Put it where you want it to be and then proceed with filling it with soil and plants.

2. You forget to pay attention to proportions ~ A large container that is filled with stunted and stubby plants is going to look awkward. A good rule to incorporate into your gardening is to try to have at least one plant that will grow as tall as your container. Once you have chosen one that will do this, you can plant other vegetation in the same container that are shorter and may even grow down the sides.

3. You drown your plants ~ Make sure your container has plenty of holes in the bottom so when you water, the excess water can drain out. Knowing when to water can be as simple as sticking your finger into the soil to see if it is dry or moist. If it feels dry to your fingertips, then it is probably time to give your plant a drink.

4. You deprive your plants of water ~ While overwatering your plant is not good, underwatering your plant is not any better. Many container gardens need watering at least once a day, especially during the summer time. For hanging plants or plants placed in small containers, they will need watering more than once a day because they have less soil to hold water and moisture. (See, I told you this could be tricky!)

5. You starve your plants ~ Potting mix is the most common ingredient used in container gardens. Unfortunately, these types of mixes don't usually contain enough nutrients for the plants to grow and flourish for the season. To compensate for the few nutrients potting mixes have, you will need to feed them fertilizers as we have discussed previously. There are many fertilizers to choose from, but the right kind will depend upon your choice of plants.

6. You are too cheap to buy good plants ~ Like everyone, you may be tempted to purchase plants you see in big box stores at cheap prices because you think they will save you money. However, cheap doesn't always mean plants in good condition. Instead, try buying excellent quality plants from reputable stores because they are often healthier plants and have smaller chances of attracting diseases and pests. Reputable stores often offer a money-back guarantee if the plants prove to be diseased or die.

7. You do not have realistic expectations ~ If you are away from home a great deal, you need to consider a self-watering system or enlist the help of a neighbor or family member. Also, consider your living style and personality.

The goal is to experiment and have fun with your garden so that you can enjoy the beauty it brings and the fun you will have growing your vegetables.

8. You are afraid to prune your plants ~ It is ironic that some plants do best when we cut off limbs. Tomato plants are like this. If you have too many branches, some of the plant's energy is expended on growing branches rather than producing fruit.

9. You fill a large container with 100% potting soil ~ If you are planning to grow shallow-rooted plants in a huge pot, try not to fill it with potting soil because it can be very expensive. Instead, fill in the bottom of the container with empty bottles, rocks or anything that can take up space. This will make the container lighter and less costly than filling it full with potting soil.

10. You use the wrong sized container ~ Container gardening is not one of the many things that you can do mindlessly or without careful planning. Do not grow shorter plants in a huge pot as it can look stunted or plant vegetable varieties in a small pot. Make sure that you choose a container with a height and size that is proportionate to the number of plants that you want to grow as well as with the size of the plant. If a crop will eventually grow tall, then choose an elongated container.

11. You use containers with little to no drainage holes ~ There are pots that are sold without holes or with a limited number of drainage holes. Refrain from using these pots because they can keep your soil too moist. This can result in rotting of the roots and death of the plant since there are no holes for excess water to drain out. Make sure you take the time to drill enough holes to let water drain out and to let the roots have room to breathe and grow.

12. You recycle unsterilized containers ~ You should not reuse your old containers without making sure they have been disinfected first. Wash the containers with soap and rinse with water or hydrogen peroxide. This will terminate bacterial growth and prevent them from infecting the plants you are planning to grow.

13. You use disease-carrying gardening tools ~ Failure to disinfect gardening tools can increase the chance of spreading pests and plant diseases. This is especially true if you have certain areas in your garden that are infested. Make sure that you thoroughly disinfect your forks, shovels, pruning shear blades, rake tongs, trowels, digging tools and other gardening equipment before you use any of them on other plants.

How Do I Prepare for Winter?

Winter time comes around every year and there are certain things you will want to think about in order to prepare your plants and containers for the cold weather.

1. Start with your containers

Glazed pots and terracotta clay pots are quite porous and can easily crack in freezing temperatures. Be sure to empty these containers, place them in a sheltered area, and position them upside down. Cover them with plastic to add extra protection to prolong the life of your containers.

2. Stop fertilizing plants during midsummer

This is one of the best ways to prepare your plants for freezing temperatures. Terminating fertilizers will reduce new growth on your plants, keeping them from being so vulnerable to frost. This is especially appropriate in plants that normally slow down their growth or become dormant when temperatures drop.

3. Consider your space and light sources

There are plants such as peppers and tomatoes that have the capacity to produce fruit even during the winter. If these plants are provided with enough light and are placed in containers that are large enough, they can be brought indoors.

4. Place potted plants into a larger container

To help plants thrive and survive cooler temperatures, place your potted plants inside larger containers. Once you do so, fill in the sides between the outside of the smaller pot and the inside of the larger pot with additional soil or mulch. This will insulate the plant's roots from the cold temperatures.

5. Bury your container in the ground

One of the things you can do to protect your plant for the winter is to bury your container in the ground. Make sure the top part of the container is on the same level with the top of the ground. If there is less soil in the container, fill it so the soil is level with the ground. Water could accumulate and freeze inside the container if it's not filled with soil.

6. Cover your plants with a generous amount of mulch

Cover the surface of your containers with mulch, especially when the soil is close to freezing. The mulch should be about two to four inches thick. Check your plant regularly and be sure to add additional mulch if necessary.

Conclusion

I hope throughout the course of this book you have become excited about the unlimited possibilities of vegetable container gardening. Here is an edible hobby and pastime that offers you creativity for your expressions as well as food for your table.

Most of all, I hope you have come to understand that you can grow vegetables in containers almost anywhere. Whether you live in a neighborhood where the yards are small or live in a high-rise apartment complex with no yard at all, vegetable container gardening offers opportunities to enjoy bountiful produce. It all comes down to knowing about containers, plants, soils, and techniques.

So, what are you waiting for? Exciting results are waiting for you in the world of vegetable container gardening. And the best part of all is that you can begin most any time of the year.

Additional Resources by Martha Green

Gardening Quick Start Guides

Container Gardening: A Quick Start Guide

Organic Gardening: A Quick Start Guide

The Green and Clean Series

Green and Clean:
Getting Started with Natural Cleaning

Green and Clean:
Natural Cleaning in the Kitchen

By Martha Green

Green and Clean:
Natural Cleaning in Bedrooms and Bathrooms

Green and Clean:
Natural Cleaning in the Laundry Room

Green and Clean:
Natural Cleaning Outside Your Home

Green and Clean:
Homemade Personal Care Products

By Martha Green

Green and Clean:
The Ultimate Collection

About the Author

Always loving the great outdoors, then graduating with a degree in environmental science, Martha thought she would spend her life working in the deepest jungles of South America. Instead, she fell in love with her college sweetheart, settled down on the west coast, and is thrilled to be a stay-at-home mom for her three great kids.

When Martha's youngest was four, she developed a severe case of asthma. After extensive medical testing and a personal quest of her own to understand why, Martha became concerned about the cleaners and products she was using in her home. Her findings have since taken her in the direction of eliminating toxins from her home, studying how to develop safe cleaning products for her family, and sharing information with her friends and family.

Although Martha never ended up in the jungle, she and her family love to go camping, hiking, boating, snorkeling and other activities that allow them to enjoy the great outdoors whenever they can.

16158969R00057

Printed in Poland
by Amazon Fulfillment
Poland Sp. z o.o., Wrocław